Why Dogs Are Better Than Men

Also by Jennifer Berman

Why Dogs Are Better Than Kids

Why Dogs Are Better Than Men

Jennifer Berman

**Andrews McMeel
Publishing**

Kansas City

ISBN: 0-7407-1405-8

Library of Congress Catalog Card Number: 00-108470

ATTENTION: SCHOOLS AND BUSINESSES

Andrews McMeel books are available at quantity discounts with bulk purchase for educational, business, or sales promotional use. For information, please write to: Special Sales Department, Andrew McMeel Publishing, 4520 Main Street, Kansas City, Missouri 64111.

FOR MATT, AND ALL THE OTHER GOOD ONES OUT THERE...

Chapter One

WHY DOGS ARE BETTER THAN MEN

DOGS LIKE YOUR SIZE

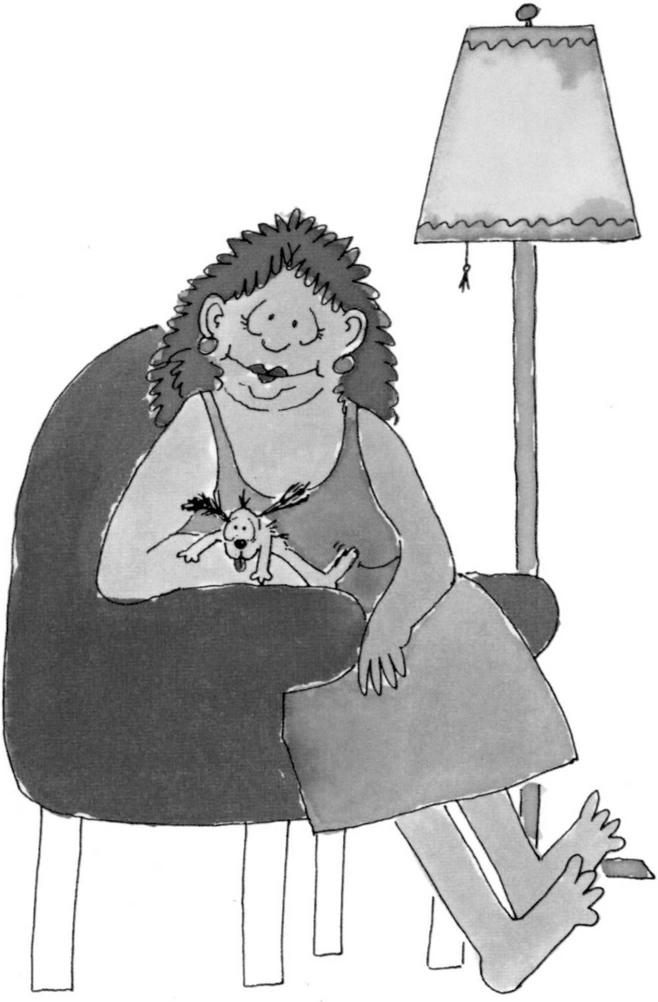

DOGS DON'T STEP ON THE IMAGINARY BRAKE

MIDDLE-AGED DOGS DON'T FEEL THE NEED TO ABANDON YOU FOR A YOUNGER OWNER

DOGS DO NOT CARE WHETHER YOU SHAVE YOUR LEGS

DOGS MISS YOU WHEN YOU'RE GONE

DOGS LOOK AT YOUR EYES

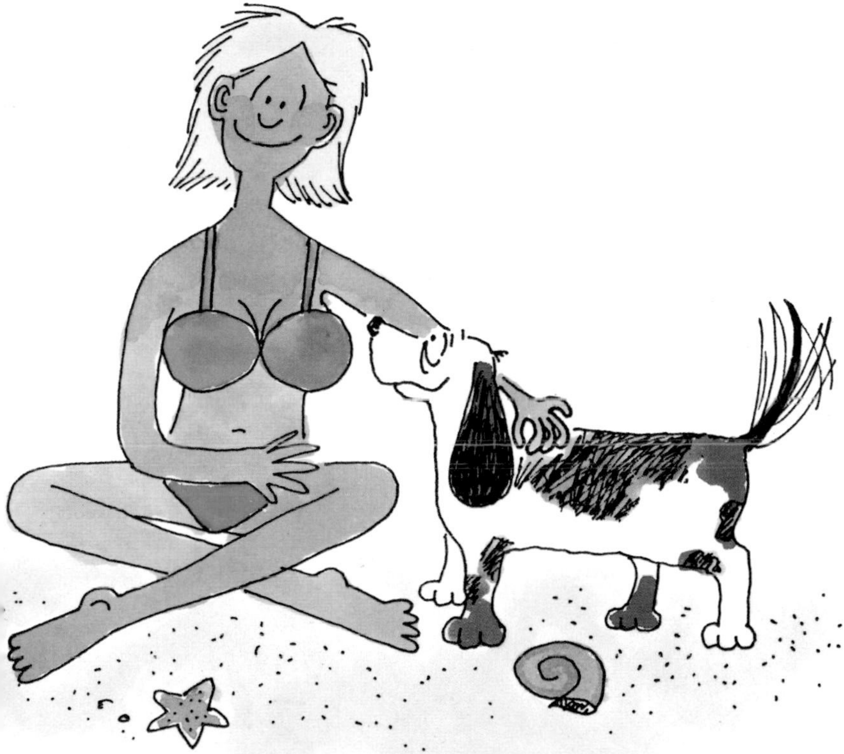

DOGS DO NOT LEAVE THE SEAT UP

YOU CAN HOUSE-TRAIN A DOG

DOGS ARE ALREADY IN TOUCH WITH THEIR INNER PUPPIES

DOGS AREN'T THREATENED BY A WOMAN WITH SHORT HAIR

DOGS AREN'T THREATENED BY TWO WOMEN WITH SHORT HAIR

DOGS ARE VERY DIRECT ABOUT WANTING TO GO OUT

DOGS ARE NICE TO YOUR RELATIVES

DOGS DON'T CORRECT YOUR STORIES

YOU CAN FORCE A DOG TO TAKE A BATH

DOGS UNDERSTAND IF SOME OF THEIR FRIENDS CANNOT COME INSIDE

YOU ARE NEVER SUSPICIOUS OF YOUR DOG'S DREAMS

DOGS DUMP **ONLY** BIODEGRADABLE WASTE

DOGS DON'T NEED THERAPY TO UNDO THEIR BAD SOCIALIZATION

DOGS ARE NOT HUNG UP ON SIZE

DOGS DON'T CRITICIZE YOUR FRIENDS

WHAT HE THINKS OF YOUR FRIENDS:
A) TERRIBLY INSECURE
B) INCOMPREHENSIBLE
C) TOO PERFECT
D) TOO CRITICAL
E) TOO AFFECTED
F) SHALLOW

WHAT YOUR DOG THINKS
A) NICE!
B) GREAT TASTE IN CLOTH
C) NICE!
D) NICE!
E) NICE!
F) NICE!

DOGS ARE COLOR-BLIND

DOGS DON'T GET DRUNK*

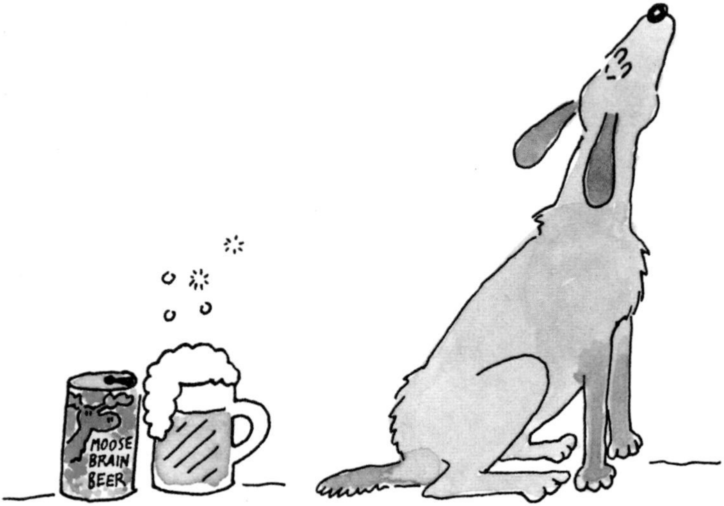
MOOSE
BRAIN
BEER

* ACTUALLY, DOGS **CAN** GET DRUNK, BUT THEY NEVE[R] USE IT AS AN EXCUSE FOR INAPPROPRIATE BEHAVIO[R]

DOGS UNDERSTAND WHAT <u>NO</u> MEANS....

DOGS ARE GOOD WITH KIDS

DOGS ARE HAPPY WITH ANY VIDEO YOU CHOOSE TO RENT, because they know the most important thing is that you're together

DOGS DO NOT PLAY GAMES WITH YOU—EXCEPT FETCH
(AND THEY NEVER LAUGH AT HOW YOU THROW)

YOU NEVER WONDER WHETHER YOUR DOG IS GOOD ENOUGH FOR YOU

DOGS DO NOT HAVE PROBLEMS EXPRESSING AFFECTION IN PUBLIC

DOGS HAVE MORE IMPORTANT THINGS TO
DO THAN WATCH THE SUPER BOWL

DOGS AREN'T THREATENED IF YOU EARN
MORE THAN THEY DO

DOGS CRY

DOGS DON'T NEED A DOGS' MOVEMENT

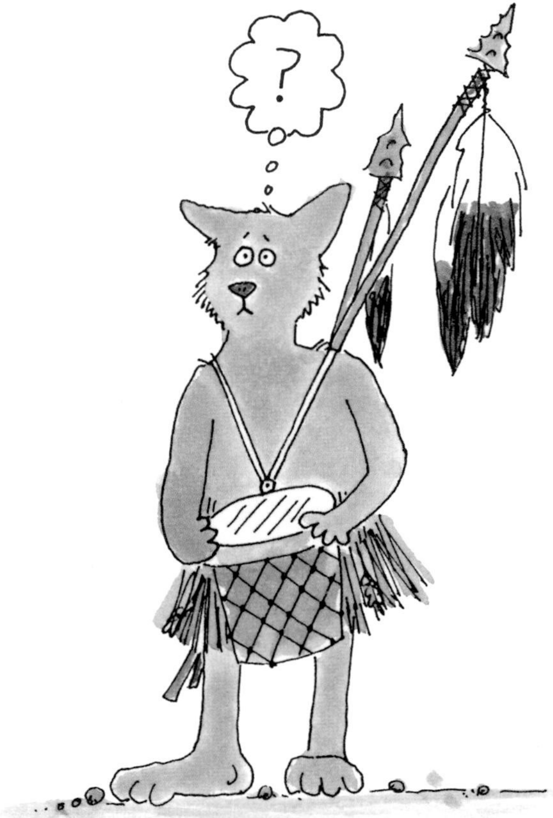
?

DOGS OWN UP TO THEIR MISTAKES

DOGS LET YOU WORK THE REMOTE CONTROL
... they're just happy to be allowed on the sofa

THE WORST SOCIAL DISEASE YOU CAN
GET FROM DOGS IS FLEAS*

OK. THE <u>REALLY</u> WORST DISEASE YOU CAN
GET FROM THEM IS RABIES, BUT THERE'S A
VACCINE FOR IT, AND YOU GET TO KILL
THE ONE WHO GIVES IT TO YOU.

GORGEOUS DOGS DON'T KNOW THEY'RE GORGEOUS

DOGS OBSESS ABOUT YOU AS MUCH AS YOU OBSESS ABOUT THEM

DOGS DON'T MAKE A PRACTICE OF KILLING THEIR OWN SPECIES

DALMATIAN   RUSSIAN WOLFHOUND   GERMAN SHEPHERD   PEKINGESE

DOGS ARE EASY TO BUY FOR

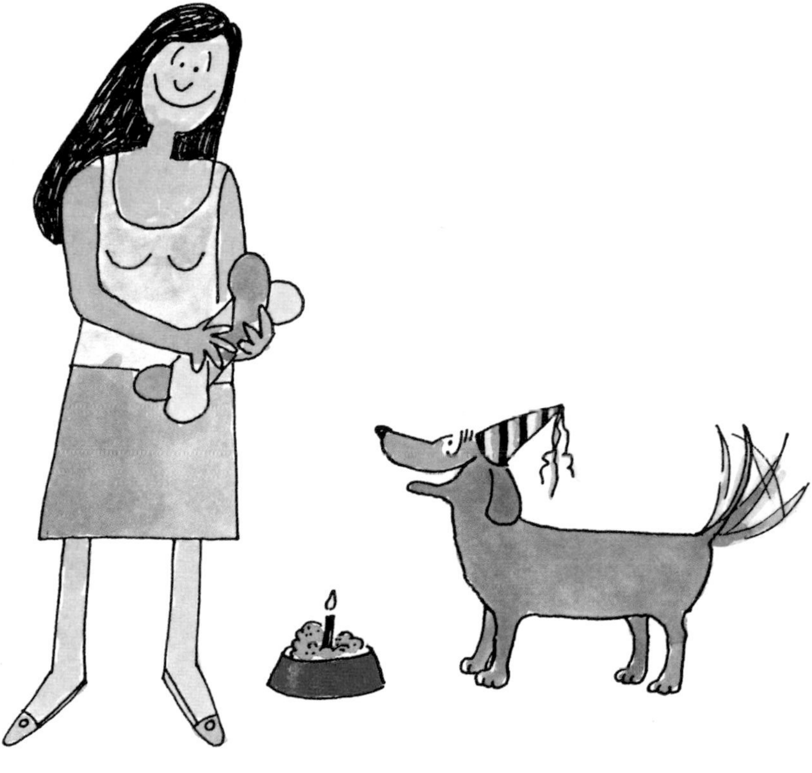

DOGS THINK YOU ARE A CULINARY GENIUS

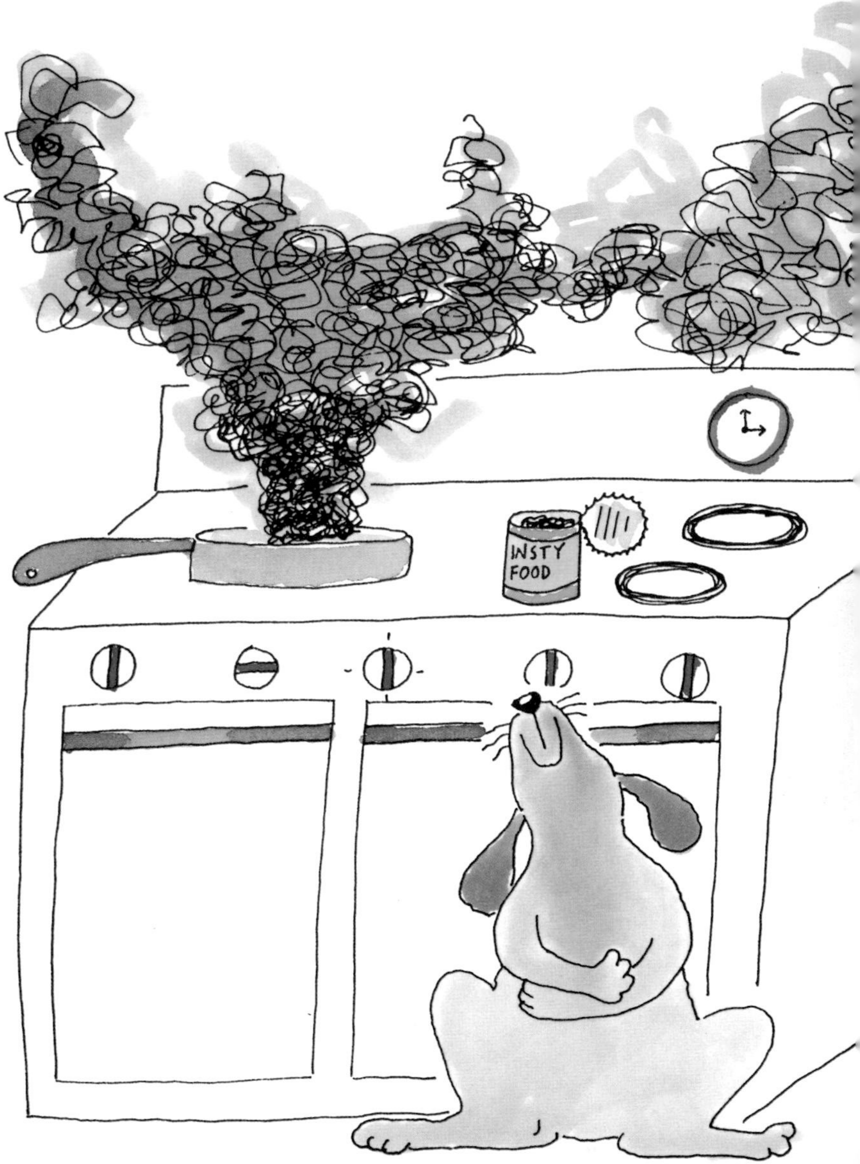
INSTY
FOOD

DOGS DON'T WEIGH DOWN YOUR PURSE WITH THEIR STUFF

DOGS DON'T MIND IF YOU DO ALL THE DRIVING

DOGS <u>MEAN</u> IT WHEN THEY KISS YOU

DOGS DON'T FEEL THREATENED BY YOUR INTELLIGENCE

DOGS FEEL GUILT WHEN THEY'VE DONE
SOMETHING WRONG

DOGS ADMIT WHEN THEY'RE JEALOUS

DOGS DON'T BRAG ABOUT WHOM THEY HAVE SLEPT WITH

DOGS TAKE CARE OF THEIR OWN NEEDS

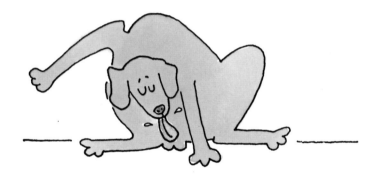

Chapter Two

HOW DOGS AND MEN ARE THE SAME

NEITHER ARE INTERESTED IN HOW YOUR DAY WAS, BUT AT LEAST DOGS DON'T PRETEND TO BE....

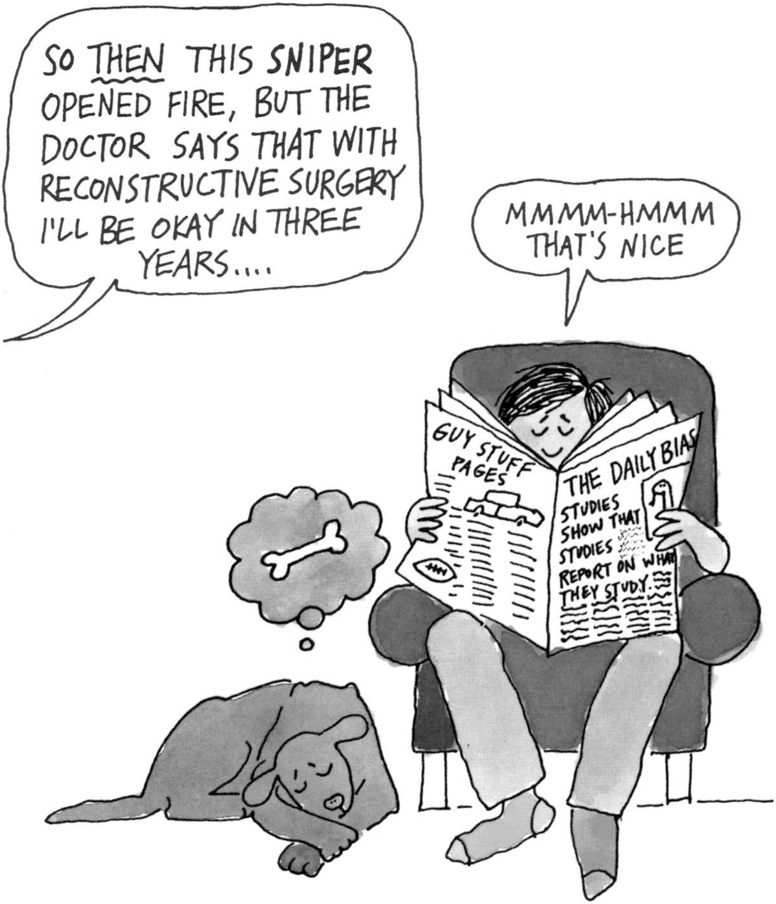
SO THEN THIS SNIPER OPENED FIRE, BUT THE DOCTOR SAYS THAT WITH RECONSTRUCTIVE SURGERY I'LL BE OKAY IN THREE YEARS....
MMMM-HMMM THAT'S NICE
GUY STUFF PAGES
THE DAILY BIAS
STUDIES SHOW THAT STUDIES REPORT ON WHAT THEY STUDY.

BOTH HAVE IRRATIONAL FEARS ABOUT VACUUM CLEANING

BOTH LOVE RELIEVING THEMSELVES IN THE GREAT OUTDOORS

NEITHER LIKES SHOPPING MUCH

BOTH LIKE CHASING AMBULANCES

MEN TAKE BETTER CARE OF FRISBEES....

....BUT DOGS MAKE MORE HEROIC CATCHES

BOTH ARE HARD ON PLANTS

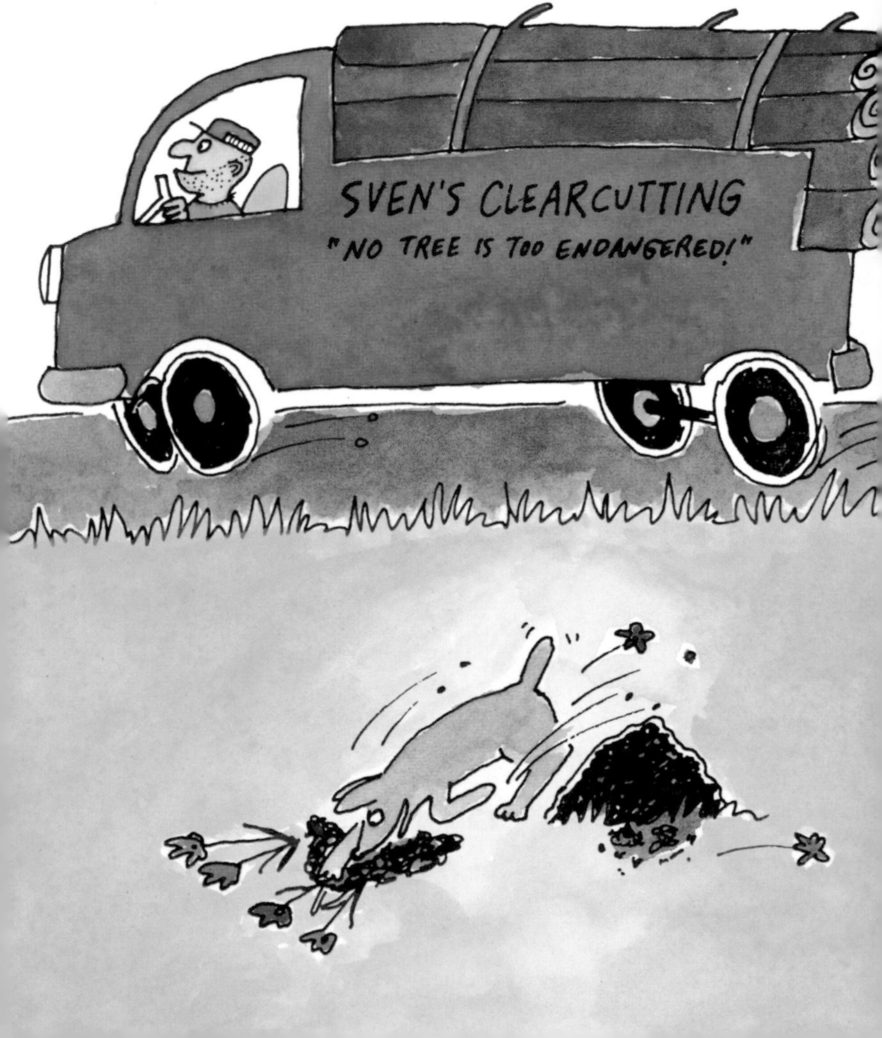
SVEN'S CLEARCUTTING
"NO TREE IS TOO ENDANGERED!"

BOTH LIKE TO TRAVEL IN PACKS

NEITHER OF THEM NOTICES WHEN YOU GET YOUR HAIR CUT....

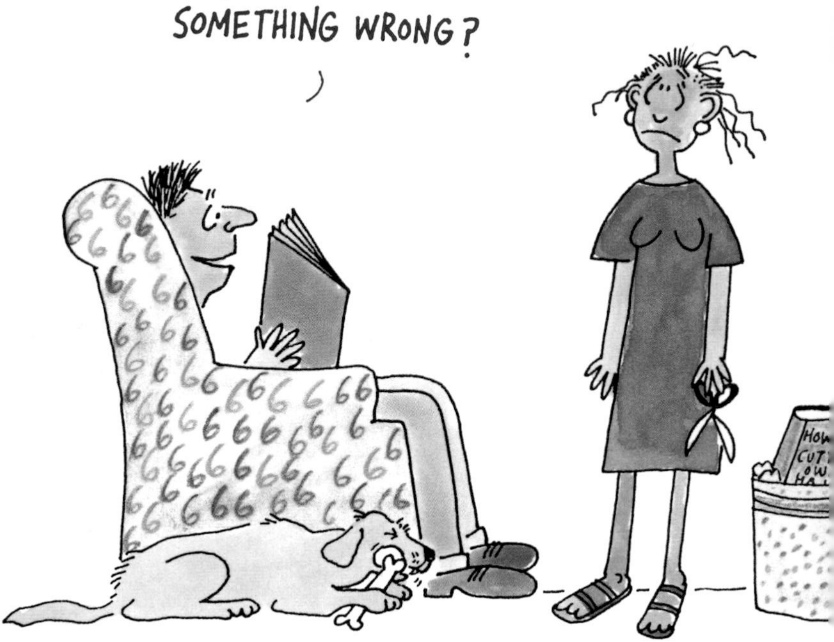
SOMETHING WRONG?

BOTH LIKE DOMINANCE GAMES

NEITHER TELLS YOU WHAT'S WRONG

BOTH TEND TO SMELL RIPER WITH AGE

BOTH HAVE AN INORDINATE FASCINATION WITH WOMEN'S PANTS

BOTH TAKE UP TOO MUCH SPACE ON THE BED

THE SMALLER ONES TEND TO BE MORE NERVOUS

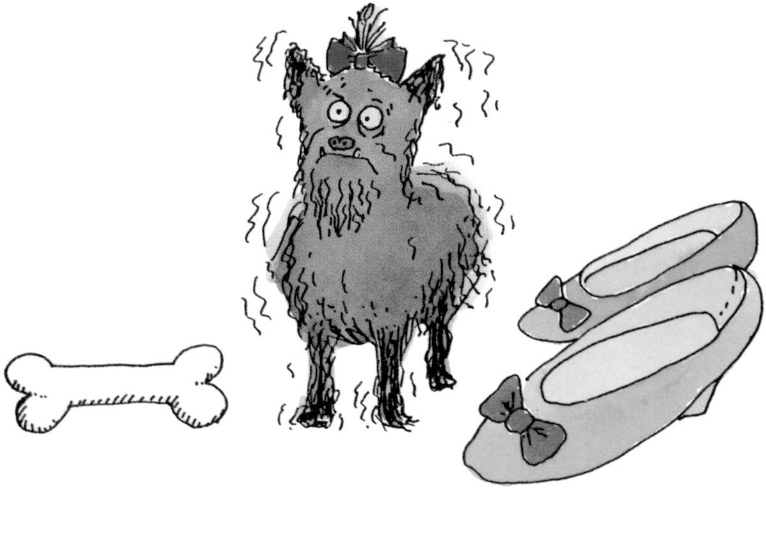

NEITHER THINKS YOU EVER HAVE TO
REPLACE FURNITURE

BOTH ARE BAD AT ASKING YOU QUESTIONS....

BOTH ARE THREATENED BY THEIR OWN KIND

BOTH LIKE TO CHEW WOOD

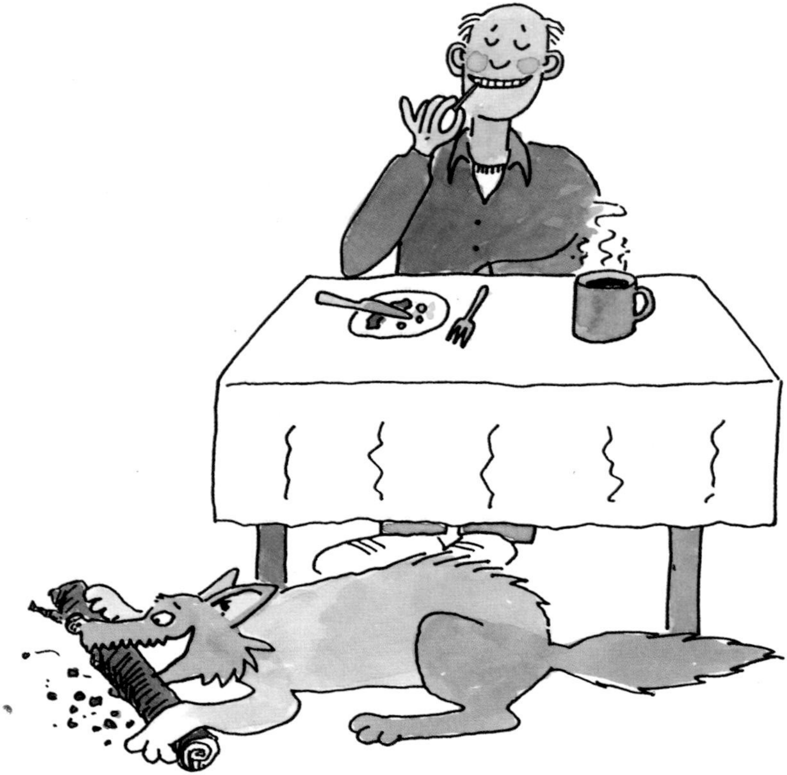

IT DOESN'T TAKE A DOG THREE HOURS TO TAKE A DUMP....

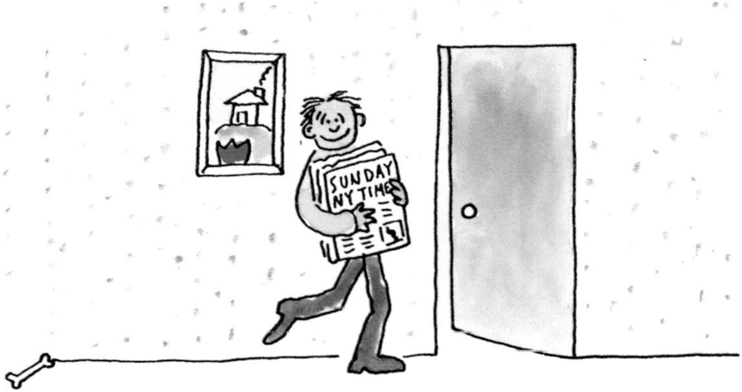
SUNDAY NY TIMES

BUT AT LEAST MEN DON'T DO IT RIGHT IN FRONT OF THE NEIGHBORS

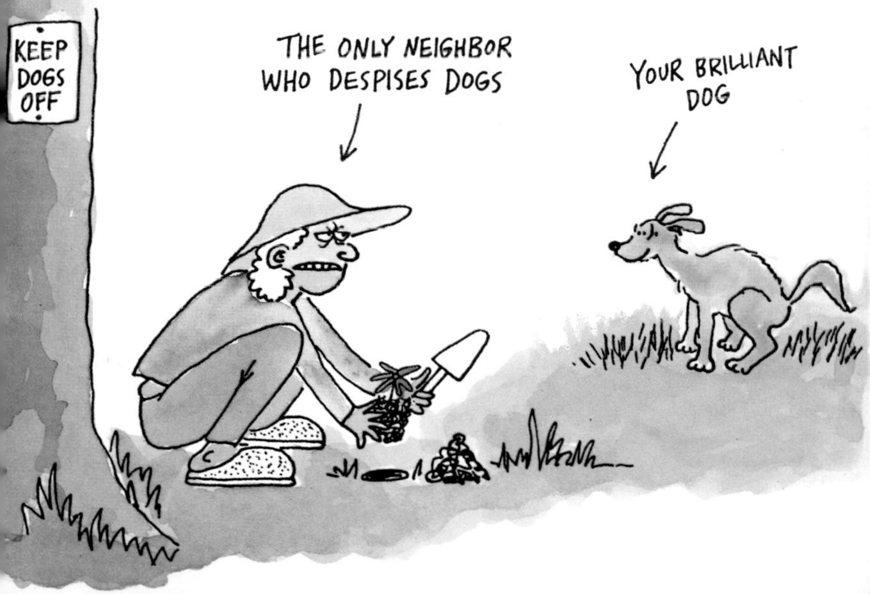
KEEP DOGS OFF
THE ONLY NEIGHBOR WHO DESPISES DOGS
YOUR BRILLIANT DOG

BOTH MARK THEIR TERRITORY

NEITHER DOES ANY DISHES

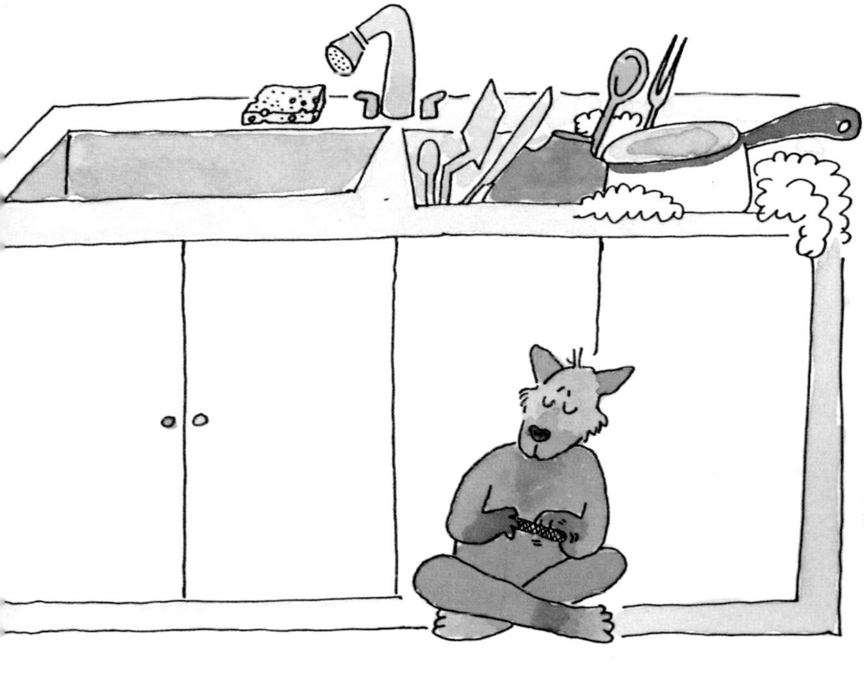

BOTH FART SHAMELESSLY

BOTH ARE SUSPICIOUS OF THE POSTMAN

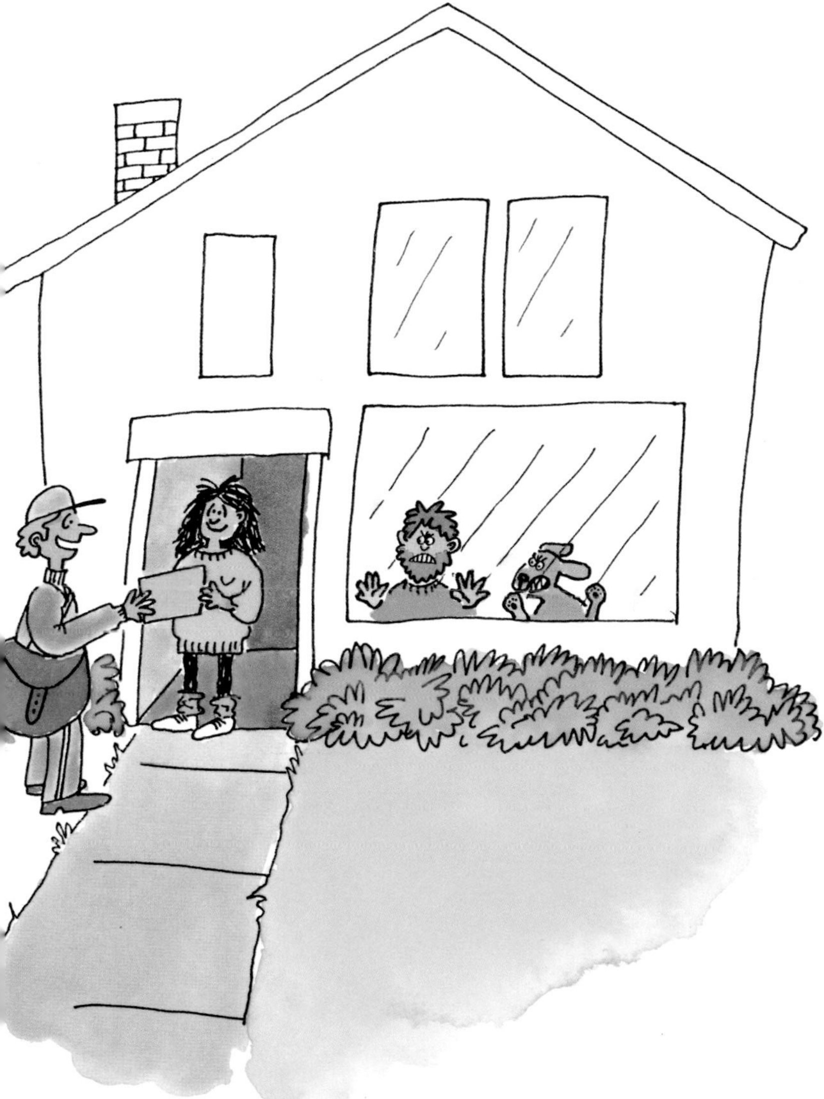

NEITHER KNOWS HOW TO TALK ON THE TELEPHONE

EITHER UNDERSTANDS WHAT YOU SEE IN CATS

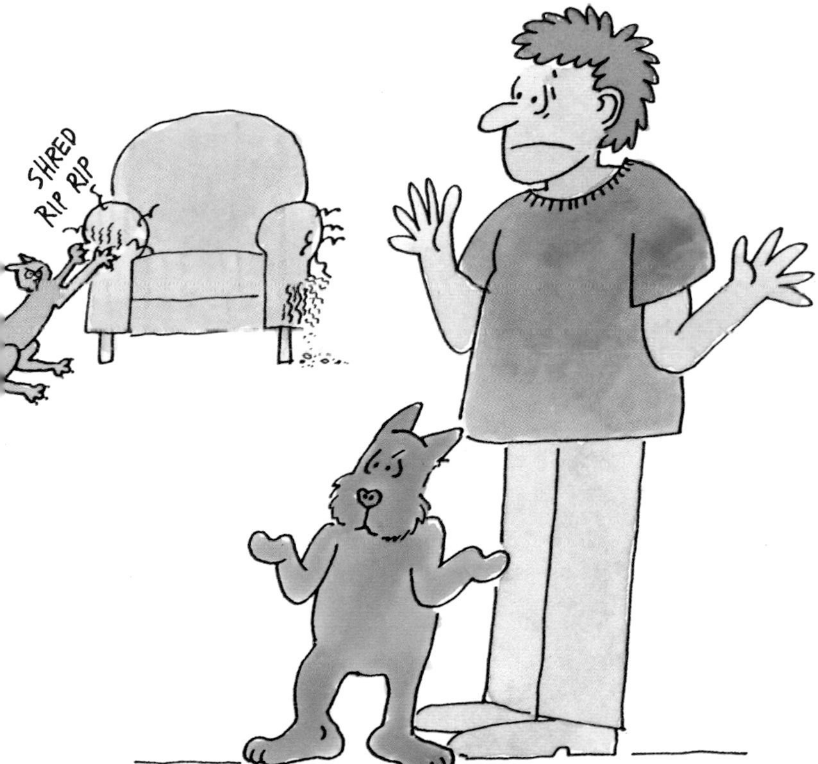
SHRED
RIP RIP

Chapter Three

WHY MEN ARE BETTER THAN DOGS

MEN HAVE SLIGHTLY BETTER CONTROL
OVER THEIR LIBIDOS

MEN ARE BETTER AT TAKING THEIR PILLS

MEN AREN'T SCARED OF THUNDER

DOGS HAVE DOG BREATH <u>ALL</u> THE TIME

MEN ONLY HAVE <u>TWO</u> FEET THAT TRACK IN MUD

MEN DON'T EAT CAT TURDS ON THE SLY

MEN CAN BUY YOU PRESENTS

MEN DON'T HAVE TO PLAY WITH EVERY MAN THEY SEE WHEN YOU TAKE THEM AROUND THE BLOCK

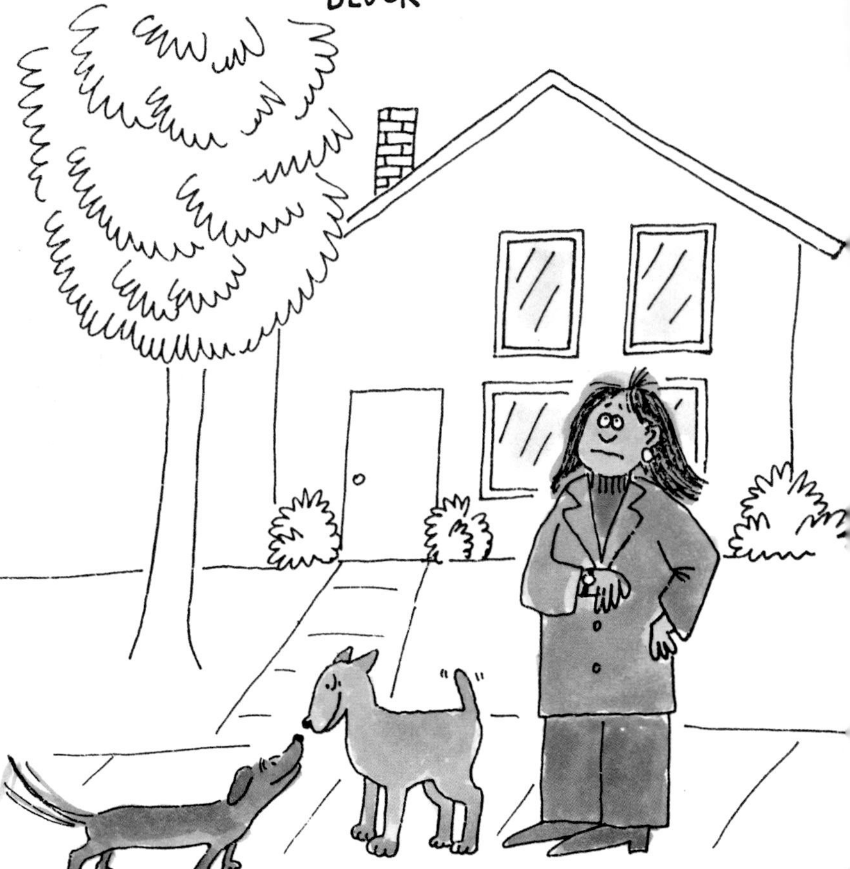

MEN OPEN THEIR OWN CANS

HOLIDAY INNS ACCEPT MEN

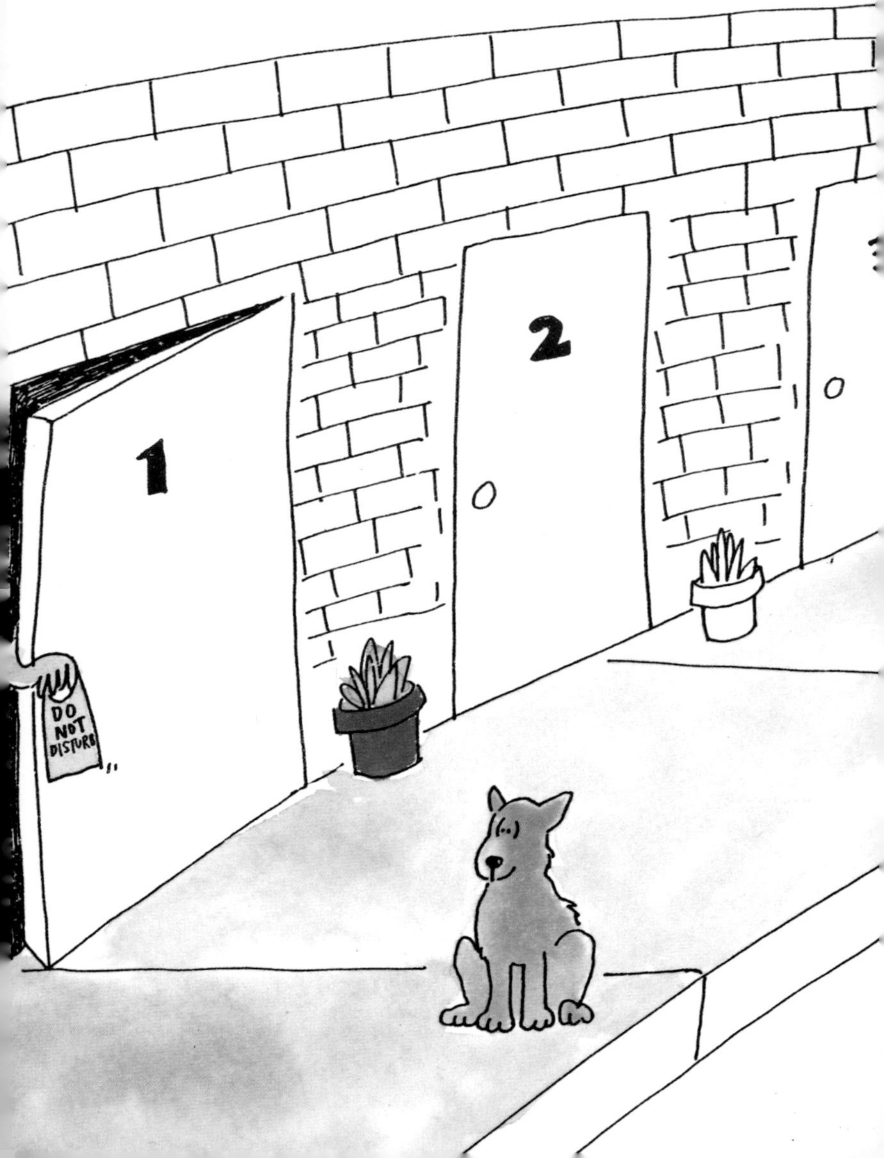

1
2
DO NOT DISTURB

MEN ARE A LITTLE BIT MORE SUBTLE

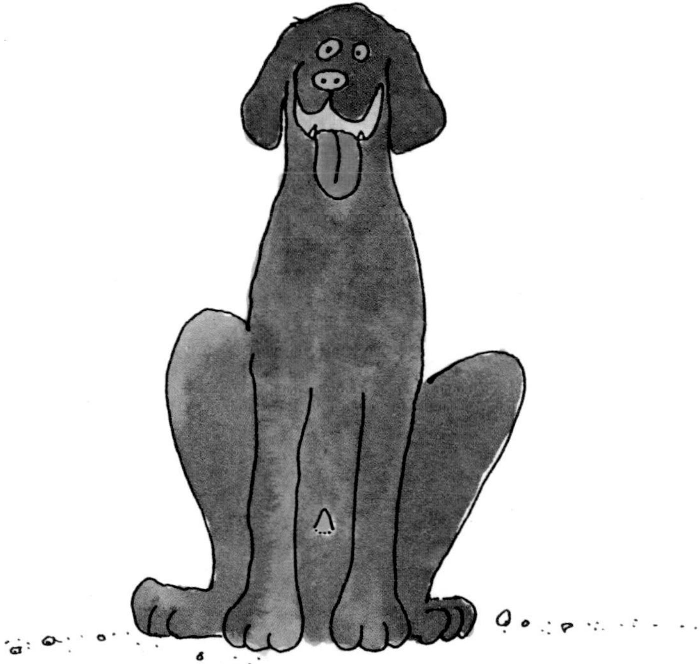

Jennifer Berman's self-syndicated cartoon panel, "Berman," appears nationally in alternative newspapers and magazines, and is syndicated internationally with Cartoonists and Writers Syndicate.

She is the author of three previous cartoon books including *Why Dogs Are Better Than Kids* and *Adult Children of Normal Parents*.

Berman is proprietor and custodian of her cartoon postcard company, Humerus Cartoons. (For more information, go to www.jenniferberman.com.)

Jennifer lives in Ohio with her husband, four dogs, and one very patient cat.